AF570327

The Body Snatchers & Other Death Rituals

by Kurt Newton

November 1, 2024

Island of Wak-Wak

Island of Wak-Wak
Örebro, Sweden
www.islandofwakwak.com

Cover Graphics: by Creative Meadow
creativemeadow.com
Used with permission.

Typeset using KOMA-Script & LaTeX 2ε.
Tryck: Libri Plureos GmbH, Hamburg,
Tyskland

ISBN: 978-91-989598-5-7

Contents

Acknowledgments

"The Accabadòra" was first published in *HWA Poetry Showcase XI* in 2024.

"Corpse Cake" was first published in *Synkroniciti* in 2022.

"Ghost Money" was first published in *Polu Texni* in 2017.

"The Body Snatchers" was first published in *Polu Texni* in 2017.

"The Cult of El Tio" was first published in *Superstitions* in 2023.

"The River Monster" was first published in *Polu Texni* in 2017.

"The Second Funeral" was first published in *Synkroniciti* in 2022.

"To Sing a Scar" was first published in *Sublimation* in 2024.

The Body Snatchers & Other Death Rituals

The River Monster

The River soothes,
the River strangles,
it rushes beneath the moon
unstoppable.

At the River's edge,
the funeral pyre rises above
our sweat stained shirts,
our calloused hands.

We drink,
we sing,
we wait
for the procession to arrive.

I cast a glance.
The River rises,
the River falls.
I know what's out there:

The River Monster,
beneath the rushing water,
with eyes of onyx,
patient as the coming dawn.

The procession approaches,
mourners cry,
prayers are spoken,
we position the corpse,

feet pointed southward,
downstream.
The River Monster
gurgles with delight.

Its odor is masked
by the scent of basil,
rose and jasmine,
sandalwood.

The chief mourner
sprinkles water,
three times he circles the pyre,
before lowering the torch.

Flames rise,
the corpse roasts and crackles.
Water splashes in the dark,
the River Monster nears.

The pyre warms the night.
We bake and bask,
we drink and sing,
thankful.

Soon the pyre crumbles,
ash and charcoal
enter the water,
hissing.

We stand back
as the River Monster
crawls ashore,
swallows the smoke

then disappears
into the River's depths,
where it will wait,
patient as the coming dawn.

The Body Snatchers

Day 1

So much noise,
so much hurry.
Tires screech and I land
like a discarded feather,
face up,
eyes toward the stars.

Motor sounds swirl,
dragging red streamers.
The air is warm,
the pavement warmer.
The night grows sharp
as the body snatchers arrive.

Faces hover.
I feel pressure,
here and there.
Their hurry dissipates.
In their eyes
I'm already dead.

I don't blame them.
How are they to know?
They are merely
collecting karma
for their next incarnation.
I'm grateful to oblige.

They wrap me in cloth,
gentle as an infant.
They offer prayers,
then lift me into a minivan.
Fingers brush across my eyes,
the night becomes permanent.

Day 2

The morgue,
as silent as a library,
as dark as a dreamless sleep.
It allows me
the necessary time
to find order in my life.

I wasn't the best husband,
the best father,
the best person
I could have been,
but in my heart
I tried.

It is said there is shame
in inaction,
to take what is given
and carelessly throw it away.
For this
I am guilty.

But I did not love any less,
I did not desire any less,
my failing
was in not knowing.
For this
I am guilty.

And though I had abandoned
everything I'd known,
and had become homeless
in every sense of the word,
I hope I leave in my absence
more than I have taken.

I hear the attendants come and go.
Bodies are removed,
bodies delivered.
It begins to smell like flowers,

flowers more fragrant than memory.
I am hopeful.

Day 3

I can no longer hear.
I merely sense the ebb and flow
of energies,
the monks from the monasteries
chanting prayers
for the lost and the damned.

It is said
when the body and brain
cease to function,
the mind is the last to depart,
the mind lingers
to ensure safe passage.

All my life
I was in a race with time.
If I didn't succeed,
or meet a certain expectation,
I thought I had failed.
I was wrong.

Time is insubstantial.
What matters is happiness.
In happiness lies all truth,
all understanding.
In happiness lies the gift of love,
to give and to receive.

The chanting enters my consciousness
in waves so perfect
it is as if I have become part
of a great chorus,
one that only the voice of death
can sing.

My eyelids become translucent.
I can see each helpful soul,
their heart beating
like a miniature furnace,
each holding a candle
to light the way home.

Most of all
I smell flowers,
beautiful potent
undying flowers,
of a scent beyond description,
beyond ethereal.

The moment approaches,
like a gentle wind.
The fragrance multiplies.
I let the wind take me.
I am at peace at last.
I fill with joy.

Ghost Money

I enter the courtyard;
there are others here,
huddled over earthenware pots
and makeshift chimneys.

The night is warm,
the air damp with the scent
of wood smoke
and the echo of a thousand prayers.

I take the bowl I carry with me,
a bowl from which my brother
ate his meals,
and place it on the ground.

In this bowl I arrange
a handful of wooden matchsticks
just so,
leaving one to light the fire.

At last, I sit.
The flames turn blond wood to brown.
I take the first wad of paper
from my pocket,

rice paper
coarse to the touch,
except where there is smooth foil
in the shape of gold bars.

I speak to the higher gods,
I tell them my brother's name,
I place the wad of paper
loosely on the fire.

My brother gambled with his life
and lost,
he left a wife and children,
an unpaid debt.

He also left an emptiness
in the hearts of those who loved him,
a vacuum in the spaces
he once occupied.

It is now upon me to save him,
to get him the money he needs
to get by on the other side,
may he use it wisely.

When the first wad burns away
I place another then another,
until my pockets are empty
and only embers remain.

I thank the higher gods,
tip the ashes onto the ground,
then stamp them cold
with the sole of my shoe.

Perhaps my brother
will buy his family
a little luck,
a streak of good fortune.

I leave the courtyard,
but I'll be back next month
and the month after,
and the month after that.

For mine is a debt
that cannot be repaid as easily
in this lifetime,
or even the next.

My brother and I fought,
until separate paths gave us
the excuse we needed
not to speak.

I gambled my brother and I
would one day be close.

I lost,
and the distance has never been so great.

The Body Breakers of Yerpa Valley

THE SMELL OF burning juniper brings the vultures out of the sky. Transformed from angels these earthbound creatures are as ugly and unapologetic as death itself. They sit along the hillside, their beaks yawning, their throats cackling unintelligible commands, while they wait for the body breakers to prepare the corpse.

Face down the naked woman is split along the back, muscle peeled away to either side. Diagonal lines are cut, exposing ribs like gills. Deep incisions down each arm, thighs and calves, to hasten the process. The vultures move even before the body breakers step away. A clumsy clamoring of wings and the feast begins.

The murmur of monks, friends and family members, the spectators who act as witnesses, is as soothing as the mountain air that rolls through the valley. Soon, the body becomes inhuman, a series of pieces bound together by ligaments and cartilage, a white birch canoe splintered on the rocks after a long and winding journey.

After the bones have been picked clean, the last morsel swallowed, the vultures once again retire to the hillside, to allow the body breakers to perform the second stage of their grisly deed. A large flat stone provides the table, a heavy mallet the proper utensil. The bones are hammered into a pinkish paste and sprinkled with millet.

The vultures watch the body breakers as the afternoon wanes. They waddle over, slower this time, weighed down by meat, in no hurry to complete the meal, a savory dessert, payment for services rendered. They nuzzle in, their eyes upon the onlookers, their wisdom no doubt able to discern the next body to grace their table.

The City of the Dead

We hiked into North Ossetia
beneath the head of Mt. Kazbek,
to a village of tiny houses on a hillside
called the City of the Dead.

We felt like giant invaders
walking among the ancient tombs,
but then the spirits of centuries past
take up very little space.

We set up camp before nightfall,
before the cold rain pelted our tents.
We had hoped to get a good night's sleep
but the ghosts were just waking up.

The first to come were the Mongols,
with the rumble of their hooves,
and the jangle of their scimitars,
to trade horses and deposit their fallen.

Next came the wails of sickness
from the plague that swept the region,
when the locals quarantined loved ones
in the crypts until they died.

This was followed by the shriek
of a girl who was kidnapped by warriors.
Legend said her captors couldn't agree
who owned her, so her throat was slit.

There were ninety-nine individual crypts,
over ten thousand souls interred,
layer upon layer of skulls and bones,
some spoke louder than others.

The equipment we brought was designed
to capture each sound and apparition,
we were students of history,
and we would bring the truth back with us.

Lastly, before dawn, we heard whispers
that circled our tents like insects.
These would be the Sarmations,
the people who had built the City of the Dead.

The Sarmations were a peaceful tribe
that had much respect for the land,
and an even greater respect for the living spirit,
even after it left the body.

When the sun at last rose in the valley,
we awoke to find one of our colleagues missing,
a female student with hair the color of fire
that the warriors of old highly coveted.

We replayed our recordings and to our dismay
not a single sound or apparition was captured.
We left the City of the Dead admonished,
our search humbly abandoned.

A Corpse in the Barn 'Til Spring

When God takes the breath
from your lungs,
whether old or young,
when the winter wind comes,
there's a corpse in the barn 'til spring.

When Death's hand knocks
on the door,
and you fall to the floor,
when the shovel can't dig no more,
there's a corpse in the barn 'til spring.

When the Devil sneaks in
from the cold,
and steals your soul,
when the night takes its toll,
there's a corpse in the barn 'til spring.

When the horned owl hoots,
and the moon turns red,
when the ground is dead
and winter spreads its wings,
there's a corpse in the barn 'til spring,
there's a corpse in the barn 'til spring.

Grave House

Those children meant
the world to me,
more so for my son
and his lovely wife,
but their passing
was too much for them,
the wound too great
to be soothed by such
a token gesture.

I was their grandfather,
their gwoppa.
My heart hurts
whenever I hear their voices—
which I often do
when I'm alone with them.
Hi, Gwoppa!
Want to play, Gwoppa?
Gwoppa, don't go.

Every Sunday,
after church service,
I hike the trail,
just me and my walking stick,
up into the hills.
The boys loved to play in those woods.
Climbing trees, picking berries,
hide-and-go-seek.

I wanted them to be protected,
kept safe from the elements,
most of all safe
from the evil spirits
that every child hears about.
Funny how folks think
it's too late to protect a loved one
once they've gone,

their duty done in this lifetime.
But what about the next?

That's why I'm the only one
who pays them a visit.
I'm old, I've seen things
a younger person
might not understand.
My son dwells too much
on the unfairness,
on the random nature
of God's plan, the cruelty
that would allow a fever
to sweep through the holler
and take not one but both boys.
The new ways didn't protect them in life,
but the old ways will in death.

I'm almost there,
I can see the twin structures
through the trees.
I get winded easily now.
There was a time
I could hike this trail
and not even think
about taking a pause along the way.
Now, I carry a walking stick
and have to stop often
just to catch my breath.

But the boys appreciate it.
It gets lonely up here on the hill.
Nothing but the wind in the trees
and the occasional cry of a hawk.
It's peaceful.
But family should stick with family,
regardless of the distance,
forgetful of the past.
When I am here,
it is only the three of us.

Hi, Gwoppa!
Hi, Gwoppa!
I smile as I sit.
I keep a chair inside the larger
of the two small houses.
I don't know if it's the wind,
or the whisper of my footsteps,
but I believe I can hear them.
They are happy to see me.
Sometimes we carry on conversations,
other times I simply sit and whittle
in silence.
My presence is what's important.

I built these miniature houses
to hold them, to comfort them,
to let them know
they are still family,
that I haven't forgotten,
that the living doesn't abandon
you once you're gone.
It's a simple favor,
one I will ask of my own son
when God takes me.

I've already drawn plans
for the house I want,
not much bigger than these,
with more windows
so I can keep a look out,
and room enough for a couple chairs,
so the whole family can come
and sit and share company.
Oh, how I will cherish eternity
with my two favorite grandchildren.

The Funeral Stripper

She moves her hips
in ways that can
stop a man's heart,
or perhaps get it
beating once again.
But she's not here
for the dead.

It's important
to this man's family
that his funeral
be well-attended.
The summer heat,
the scent of death,
makes for an
unattractive draw.

So, there's music,
food and drink,
a festive atmosphere
to bring prestige
to one who will perhaps
be celebrated more
in death than in life.
But they're not here
for the dead.

They're here for her,
she who gives birth,
she who nurtures
with mother's milk,
she who offers sex
and beauty and the
promise of something
beyond: a future
that will stretch
several lifetimes,
if not more.

So, these men,
and some women,
who ogle her,
their brains doused
with alcohol,
heartbeat strong,
loins on fire,
while their mates
cast aspersions,
know full well
who the funeral
stripper is really for.

Her lithe body
and shimmery dress,
her darting tongue
on painted lips,
is but a reminder
that life is as fleeting
as a snake in the grass,
and we must love
while we can,
dance while we can,
because the ground
beneath us can shift
at any moment.

The Second Funeral

The elderly woman sits
in quiet repose,
she can do no else,
as this was her last act before dying,
and yet she is not dead.
Her family has seen to it.
This great grandmother,
this grandmother,
this mother, daughter, wife,
this fixture for generations,
may no longer have air in her lungs,
a heartbeat in her chest,
or that spark in her eye
her loved ones knew so well,
but she is alive still,
as long as her family refuses
to let go.

Today is her second funeral,
the first was eight months ago
when she stopped moving,
found in her favorite chair
by one of her grandchildren.
But it is the way of this village,
these people,
who have no fear of death,
in fact, they live for death,
it is the way of the ancestors.
Living here among the coffee trees
and the bougainvillea,
on stilted houses standing knee-deep
in a sea of thick green palm,
they welcome death as one would
an old friend.

Today the word has spread.
Today the villagers will come
and family from distant places.

Today the air will fill
with squealing pigs,
the bellow of water buffalo,
the rev of motorcycle vendors,
the catcalls from women
in tight dresses
selling cigarettes.
Today is the culmination
of eight months of receptions,
prayers and sitting with the family
at the dinner table,
the scent of formalin
masked by sandalwood.
Today is not the end
but only the next petal
in an ever-unfolding flower.

Today she will be moved
out of the home to one of the many
ancestral buildings that hug the hillside.
Later on, she will be moved
to a rice barn, where she will sit
and preside over the food
she cooked so well.
And, eventually,
she will be moved again,
to the funeral tower that
overlooks the ceremonial plain.
This process could take years,
if not decades, to evolve,
each time the distance growing
in gentle increments
to allow the bonds of love
to extend
into the afterlife.

The Bog People

Some say this land
was once a gateway
to the spiritual world,
but I saw nothing
but weed and mud.

My brother and I
were cutting peat,
to dry for fuel
for the coming winter,
when the body appeared.

It was cocooned
several feet deep
as if asleep
in the rich, dark earth,
a rope around its neck.

Our first thought was to
ignore what we had found
and move on, we didn't
want any part of any crime
we weren't guilty of.

But our better natures prevailed.
It would have been a crime
to leave that man alone,
now exposed, awakened
by our shovel's blade.

The police uncovered
more bodies, more souls
trapped within the bog.
My brother and I
volunteered our backs.

A University scientist
dated the remains to the Iron Age:
a sacrificial king,

a ceremonial execution,
a slaughtered outcast.

It was a primitive time,
one of ritual and superstition.
It wasn't until we found
the girl with the flaming hair
that I began to question my beliefs.

She was young, no older
than my teenage daughter.
She had been strangled
with a woolen belt
and stabbed in the heart.

The Strangled Adulteress,
they dubbed her,
a she-devil
in Medieval times,
executed for infidelity.

Soon after, my brother
began acting strangely,
affected by the digging,
the revealing,
the ugly truths buried deep.

I began to see him
like a ghost around town,
glimpsed from a distance,
arm in arm with a girl
with flaming hair.

When he disappeared
for almost a week,
the authorities were called.
No one had seen him,
and only I seemed to care.

He was found in the bog
face down in the mud

by a University student.
Accidentally drowned, they said
after a night of drinking.

I realized then that all of us
will end up in the ground,
one way or another,
if not by someone else's hand
than most surely by our own.

To Sing a Scar

It is said she lives in the woodland wild,
alone with the sorrows of losing a child,
    a long head of hair she is always combing,
    her mournful cry carried in the air in the gloaming.

Tis a brutal dance of death eternal,
between the heavenly light and dark infernal,
    to sing a scar upon the living
and carry its memory home,
    to sing a scar upon the living
and bury the blood and the bone.

When death has passed its iron will,
she cuts a path through field and hill,
    a primal song of fur and feather
    to guide the soul into the aether.

Tis a brutal dance of death eternal,
between the heavenly light and dark infernal,
    to sing a scar upon the living
and carry its memory home,
    to sing a scar upon the living
and bury the blood and the bone.

When the sun has set and the soil tamped,
she returns to the wild to mourn again,
    borne on the wind you can hear her keening,
    for the child for which her soul is bleeding.

Tis a brutal dance of death eternal,
between the heavenly light and dark infernal,
    to sing a scar upon the living
and carry its memory home,
    to sing a scar upon the living
and cherish the flesh and the bone.

The Ballad of Stuckie

This is the ballad of Stuckie,
a hunting dog not dumb but unlucky,
a dog with a singular purpose in mind:
to rid the world of every squirrel he could find.

One day, Stuckie was following his nose,
marking his territory near a chestnut tree grove,
when a grey blur caught the corner of his vision,
and off he ran like a dog on a mission.

He chased that squirrel first this way then that,
across dead slippery leaves and dew-damp grass,
the squirrel was agile, nimble and fast,
but Stuckie had it cornered, at last.

He'd chased that squirrel to a hollowed-out tree,
where it disappeared down a hole where the roots used to be.
In Stuckie dove, into the rotted-out breach,
the squirrel scrambling for purchase just out of reach.

Inside the bole, Stuckie dutifully climbed,
lunging for his quarry one final time,
but space had run out, along with his luck,
and Stuckie became irretrievable stuck.

The squirrel escaped and night came to the grove,
Stuckie stuck in the tree, in the dark, all alone,
his bark strangled and muffled and lost on the wind
when he heard his master's voice calling for him.

For days, Stuckie tried to reverse his fate,
but the more he struggled, the more stuck he became,
until the cold and the pain and all his troubles went away,
and he was back home curled up close to the fireplace.

Of course, Stuckie's name wasn't Stuckie then,
it was fifty years before he saw sunlight again.
A chainsaw nearly cut Stuckie in half, truth be told,
when loggers took down the old chestnut grove.

And there was Stuckie, a dog mummified,
bound and determined till the day he died,
a snarl on his lip, teeth bared, steely eyed,
chasing squirrels forever in the afterlife.

Stuckie's now on display in a forest museum,
an inspiration to any and all who see him,
frozen in time on his own wild hunt:
Stuckie, the dog that never gave up.

The Merry Cemetery

The Merry Cemetery
is a Mardi Gras for mourners.
Wooden crosses painted
with the colors of the dead.
Red for passion,
yellow for fertility,
green for life,
and blue for hope and freedom.
Black, of course, for death.
There are many blackbirds
in the Merry Cemetery,
painted in the cross's wings,
as if waiting their cue to take the stage.
There are very few doves
in the Merry Cemetery,
doves as white as communion dresses,
for these represent the very rare
and often maligned soul that's pure.
Sometimes there's a pet,
a dog or cat if the deceased
was loved more by their animal
than their own family.
Fish for fishermen,
crochet needles and yarn
in a fanciful skull and crossbones
for seamstresses,
a musical instrument
if one provided a modicum of joy
to their listeners.
The Merry Cemetery
sits in the heart of a small village,
and like any small village
everyone knows everybody,
and everybody's business.
Secrets are the first to die
once the body is in the ground.
Adulterers are portrayed
in an embarrassing light,

one foot in matrimony,
the other in a fiery hell.
The obese are sometimes
presented as jolly hogs,
drunkards as court jesters
and politicians as fools.
To make light of such a thing
as one's demise,
the cross maker must surely
be despised in the village,
and yet, in the Merry Cemetery
tears are better spent
on the living,
and never wasted on the dead.

Ode to the Deathwatch Beetle

Poor beetle, lowly bug of death and dying,
what a cruel, unjust mistake!
Tap, tap, tap — the Grim Reaper is coming, there's no denying,
when all the beetle is trying to do is attract a mate.

It chews into the woodwork with a syncopated tick,
as if a clock is counting down the moments left.
It knows not of superstition or who in the household may be sick,
it simply knows to bore a hole and bang its head.

Tap, tap, tap — a message to all females who might be near,
a rhythmic signal of copulation sent.
The irony is lost on those who choose to live in fear,
allowing death to commandeer the way our time is spent.

Poor beetle, lonely bug of death and dying,
so underappreciated, so misunderstood!
Perhaps to live to love is all we should be trying
to do before the Reaper comes and sweeps us beneath his hallowed hood.

Mummia

Goodnight my sweet Prince
May our love know no bounds
in this life and in the one that comes after . . .

The face of Anubis loomed over the peasant girl
as she took her final breath.
Such beauty, the embalmer thought
as he sliced open her belly
and removed her internal organs.

Goodnight my sweet lotus flower
May the fragrance of our love carry
to the four corners and beyond . . .

The Prince lay beside the peasant girl;
the two held hands, assuming the sleep of the dead.
A hook was inserted into the Prince's nose
and, piece by piece, the embalmer
removed his brain.

Such scandal!
The Prince and his peasant girl,
meeting along the banks of the Nile,
the Prince disguised as a boatman.
The Prince's uncle, the King,
would rather his nephew marry an enemy's daughter,
than an enemy of good breeding.
Death! Death to the peasant girl!
Death to her parents for producing
such a powerful enchantress!
But the Prince was in love,
a love truer than any throne that could be promised.
If he couldn't have his true love in this life
he would have it in the next.
Under a crescent moon they departed,
hand-in-hand into the afterlife.

What in the name of Isis?
Where am I? Why do I see through aging eyes?
Who is that on the table? My Prince?
What are they doing to you?

The powder she ingested earlier
appeared to be having its desired effect.
Her joints barely ached,
her eyesight was clearer.
It could have been the wine served
at the start of this Unwrapping Party,
but there was a curious whispering in her ears.
Who knew there could be a medicinal benefit
from ground mummified remains?

What in the name of Osiris?
Who is this brutish gang that stands witness
to my desecration? My love? I feel you near.
Where is my lotus flower?

The surgeon peeled the layers
from the ancient carcass, pausing now and then
to provide descriptive monologue to the audience,
adding suspense to the spectacle.
An older woman approached the table;
before anyone could stop her,
she reached out and grasped the mummy's hand.
Her face exhibited a heavenly aura
just before she fainted.

There you are my beautiful one
I told you we would be together
Not even death can keep us apart

My Prince, my love, I am here
Hold me, hold me now and never let go
My Prince? What is happening?

I fear the chain has been broken
Goodbye my love, till we meet again
my heart will forever be with you

My sweet Prince, don't go! Don't leave me
This cannot be the end, I will find you
However long it takes, I will find you

A process several thousand years in the making
was over in the wink of an invisible eye.
Adrift, the spirits of the Prince
and the peasant girl, wafted and swirled
like smoke from a ceremonial censer,
together and yet apart
they rose into oblivion.

Corpse Cake

It is still dark when Grandma Lemke rises.
She boils the wheat.
Her brother, Olaf, lies in the next room.
She kneads the dough with arthritic hands,
firmly, lovingly,
pressing, stretching, folding
until her muscles burn.
At last, she shapes the dough
into a miniature burial mound
and places it upon her brother's linen-wrapped chest.
Grandma Lemke rests
until the sun comes up.

When the dough has risen,
extracting the good and the bad,
a lifetime of virtues,
a lifetime of sins,
Grandma Lemke removes it from Olaf's chest.
He is now in good hands.
The dough is then placed in the oven
where it bakes and hardens,
the flavor, the essence of her brother
trapped within.
When cooled, she sprinkles the cake with sugar,
adds nuts and dried fruit to make it palatable.
She tears the cake in two
and places it once again on her brother's body.

By now, family has gathered around the patriarch,
along with a bearded stranger,
a rank and devilish-looking man
by the name of Gotz.
No one stands close to Gotz
and no one dare speak to the repulsive man,
who eyes the cake with a child-like fervor.
Grandma Lemke lifts one half of the cake
and says a prayer, she takes a bite,
tasting her brother's kindness.

The cake is then passed among family,
distributing Olaf's talents and wisdom.
His skill with an ax to young Bruno,
his penchant for fiddle playing to Inga,
his sense of humor to Magnus,
his curiosity to Yvonne.

Then all eyes turn toward the stranger.
Grandma Lemke nods
and Gotz grabs the other half of the cake
for himself.
It is devoured within minutes
in an orgy of teeth and lips and saliva.
The greed the gluttony,
the sloth and the lust,
the wrath and the envy,
and, at last, the pride.
Fruit and nuts and sugary crumbs—
all gone. Fingers licked,
beard sifted through for remnants.
Gotz is thanked then shown the door.

A joyousness fills the void.
There are songs and remembrances,
laughter and more food.
There is drink and dancing.
Even Grandma Lemke allows a smile.
Her brother may have left them
but he has left much in his departure.
His sons and daughters,
his grandchildren.
There is even a great-grandchild
swimming in Hanna's womb.
It is time to celebrate.
Death has left them . . .
at least, for now.

The Cult of El Tio

Basilio lives in two worlds:
the world that exists outside the mine—
where he worships God with his family
every Sunday in the little church
that sits at the foot of Cerro Rico,
and the world that exists inside the mine,
inside the Mountain That Eats Men—
where God cannot enter,
where El Tio sits eyeing the workers
who dig for silver in the mountain's stomach
chipping away like a cancer,
measuring their faith in the offerings they bring,
deciding each day who walks out into the evening sun—
face and hands dirty, lungs coughing thick phlegm, but alive—
and who stays, buried in the latest cave-in,
eaten by stone teeth.

Today, Basilio brings hand-rolled cigarettes.
He places a half dozen beside El Tio,
takes one and lights it,
inhaling a lungful of sweet tobacco smoke
before wedging the cigarette between El Tio's lips.
"For you, my friend," Basilio whispers into El Tio's ear
before hurrying away to begin his job.
There is a line behind him,
fellow workers with offerings of *puro*—
a potent alcohol the men drink throughout the day—
trinkets, coca leaves, and llama blood.
The horned creature takes it all,
sitting naked on his makeshift throne,
face sporting fish eyes and a devilish grimace,
his large manhood pointed upward
toward the low ceiling.

The Cult of El Tio.
The village clergy frown upon such heresies,
but they understand the need:
when entering Hell, one must appease

the demons that dwell there.
And there are many demons inside Cerro Rico,
many demons outside as well—
the mine bosses, the child laborers,
the mercury used to suck the silver from the stone,
the drug lords who rule the village streets
with beatings and beheadings.
For Basilio, sometimes the safest part of his day
is entering the mine, kissing El Tio's feet,
thanking him for another day of foul breath,
while, little by little, both God in Heaven
and the Devil in the earth
extract the silver from his soul.

The Cloud Warriors of Kuelap

"THE DEAD ARE watching," says Alejandro. Alessa looks up and sees the white-faced sarcophagi standing along the cliff face that rises high above Lagunas de Los Condores. She unties her bathing suit top and tosses it aside. "Let them watch," she says and dives into the cool lake water.

How the mummified remains of their ancestors and their stone tombs came to be perched like condors on the steep hillside is still a mystery. It is told that powerful shaman of the time possessed the ability to levitate not just themselves but anyone or anything the shaman deemed worthy of the effort.

As Alessa and Alejandro swim in the lake below, splashing each other playfully, the mummies look on, their eyes sealed behind wraps of fine cloth, their feathers and jewelry looted long ago: Cloud Warriors who once ruled and gave their life to protect the Fortress in the Sky. From whom? Or from what?

The answer lies in Lagunas de Los Condores, on the bottom of its 60-meter depth, a depth too murky to pierce with human eyes. Alessa and Alejandro finish their swim and stretch their youthful bodies on towels, bathing in the afternoon sun, as the Cloud Warriors continue to watch, their secrets kept hidden.

The Jade Suit

It was a tall order.
Although the Emperor's head
topped no higher than the back of a riding horse,
his essence projected a man
much greater in size than his physical stature.
As with all supreme leaders
it was not the width of his fists
but the measure of his heart
and the depth of his love for his people
that set him above the rest.

The Emperor was patient
as our fitters flitted like butterflies,
measuring every length and width
and circumference,
producing a three-dimensional diagram
of a man who was no doubt
measuring the distance of his life,
the reach of his power
and the size of his legacy.
It was now my responsibility
to preserve the essence of the Emperor
in a very special suit.

Jade from the quarries in Ningshao
was delivered and our craftsmen
selected only the best quality
for each and every piece.
They worked tirelessly
beginning when the Emperor was a young man,
during wartime and famine,
for ten years cutting and polishing,
the skin on their fingers
permanently tinted by pale, green dust.

1547 pieces for the Emperor's torso,
1932 pieces to cover his arms and legs,
211 pieces for his hands and feet,

306 pieces for his face and head.
3996 pieces in total,
squares and rectangles,
triangles and circles,
the number itself a sign of good luck
and good fortune in the afterlife,
all grouped by placement
on the Emperor's anatomy,
like tokens used for gambling,v each the color of green tea
and possessing the luster of pearl and silk.

The Emperor was a strong believer
in the power of jade
and its protective properties.
The suit would one day deliver his soul
into the Paradise of Immortals.
He believed so strongly,
he drank an elixir made from the powdered stone.
He drank it every morning when the sun rose
and every evening when it set,
in a symbolic act of continuity.
But, over time, he fell ill,
which prompted him to drink even more.
But the more he drank
the more ill he became.
Toward the end, we had to hurry.
We finished the suit
on the eve of his death.

As the Emperor lay dying,
he ordered us to prepare him,
he didn't want eternity to escape his grasp.
Section by section, he was dressed,
assembled the way one might assemble a doll,
with joints at the shoulders, the hips,
the wrists and ankles, the neck,
each joint then sewn together with threads of gold.
A special face plate had been made,
a likeness both regal and kind,
this was left off until the Emperor

exhaled his last breath,
and then his body was sealed inside the jade.

A superstitious person might believe
the two events were linked.
If the Emperor hadn't ordered the suit,
perhaps he would still be alive?
Perhaps to give up one's fight against death
is to invite death to deliver its fateful blow?
No matter,
the jade suit was designed to provide immortality.
The Emperor's body may no longer be extant
but his essence lives on,
in his achievements, his legacy,
in the eyes of all who now view him,
forever enshrined within the stone.

Dead Yard

In the village, a living soul becomes a death soul, for nine days
it lingers, hovering, circling like the shadow of a black vulture,
the grave is dug and the waiting begins

Whispers of the death soul's name are carried on the breeze and
deposited in the ear like a hummingbird dipping its beak for
nectar in the orange flowers of the sanchezia

Meanwhile friends and family gather around the deceased, their
tears wringing out the grief they've stored, in the hut they mourn,
the body wrapped from head to toe, a life-sized dolly

A celebration need not be planned, the whispers bring flowers
and gifts and food and drink and liquor and ice from all over
the island in a steady flow of familiar strangers

Some bring music, some bring dominoes, others bring just
their smiles, their words of hope and kindness, all bring a sense
of loss and newfound appreciation for life

The soul of grief dances with the soul of happiness, the way the
breeze dances with the trees, the way the ocean water dances
with the sandy beach, and the island sings along

Memories are shared and stories told like miniature movies
projected on the night air, the alcohol flows until the death soul
becomes a living soul again, momentarily reborn

A vigil is kept inside the hut, the life-sized dolly doesn't move,
but if eyes are taken away or fall into a dream, perhaps the
hut will be empty when the watcher awakens

The final meal is prepared, a slaughtered pig roasted through
the night, goat soup and cooked green bananas, while children
dressed in white chase each other like ghosts

On the ninth night the body is moved, the bed stood on end,
the death soul is asked to leave the empty hut, and when it does,
a cross is drawn in white chalk above the doorway

The death soul circles frantic, it tries to enter every breathing
mouth, but each knows its name and cannot be tricked, and so
it has nowhere else to go but into the open grave

The lid is placed upon the coffin, to bring closure to a life,
to seal in the bad spirit with the dead meat of the body,
the grave is filled, leaving only the good behind

The Accabadòra

he is dying
writhing in pain like a snake caught in a hawk's talons
he speaks to those who are not there
his cheeks are streaked with the crust of tears

it is time
send word to the Accabadòra
tell her the door has been left open

the Accabadòra enters dressed in black
moving like a fog
Lady of the Good Death
The One Who Ends

a large hammer made of olive wood
its head wrapped in heavy wool
is carried at her side

she is drawn to the agonizing sounds
the way a cormorant is drawn to the sea
she moves into the candlelit bedroom
and begins to sing

a soothing lullaby
like one remembered from childhood
forehead slick with fever
a mother's hand cool to the touch

calming quieting relaxing
before the hammer is raised
then brought down with the might of God

the Accabadòra leaves
the way fog is swallowed by daylight
the old man who was once a mother's infant son
lying silent in her wake